Two Elk
A High Country Notebook

Andrew Schelling

The Positively Past Post-Modern Poet Series #3

BOOTSTRAP PRESS
LOWELL, MASSACHUSETTS

Front Cover Art: "Two Elk Burning: Vail, CO" by Derek Fenner. Digitally manipulated photographic assemblage.

Back Cover Calligraphy: "Beauty" by Marlow Brooks. Sumi ink and pastel, created with a pine needle brush.

Author drawing: Derek Fenner, "Schelling," pencil & ink, 14" x 17", 2005.

Sections of *Two Elk: A High Country Notebook* have been published by *Bombay Gin*, *sliding uteri, Small Town*, and *the @tached document 3*. The Preface and other sections appeared in *Gasping for Air in a Vacuum: Poems and Prayers to Yogi Ramsuratkumar*, Hohm Press, 2004. Thanks to the editors and readers of these publications.

ISBN 0-9711935-4-1

Bootstrap Press Books are designed and edited by Derek Fenner and Ryan Gallagher and published at Bootstrap Productions, 82 Wyman Street, Lowell, MA 01852.

THIS IS A BOOTSTRAP PRODUCTION!

www.bootstrapproductions.org

*This book is dedicated to
Althea Schelling & Marlow Brooks.*

PREFACE

During autumn of 2003 I kept a high country journal which I eventually named *Two Elk* after the creek that lies in an adjacent drainage to Vail ski resort's Category III expansion. My project in the notebooks was to document excursions into Colorado's high altitude terrain. These formidable peaks & high valleys—with their low oxygen, scant moisture, intense sunlight, scouring winds, & tough ice—have been my kindest, toughest, & sturdiest teachers the fourteen years I've lived among them. Hence the notebook entries became songs, prayers, and poems of devotion. Standing on the expression-filled granite brow of a mountain, or carrying on life near its feet, moments of spontaneous song would come over me. Already in 1998 this had appeared—

> These slow-leaning schist
> & granite mountains,
> their learned heads.

But dream world distortions began to enter the notebook too, and with the strange displacements of dream-time my posture of respect often took on odd, ironic, or ambivalent tones. At times this made the praise-songs reminiscent of India's curious tradition of *ninda stuti*.

Ninda stuti—ironic praise; "praise in the form of abusive reproach." I learnt the taste of it first through the poems of the peerless 18th century Bengali poet Ramprasad Sen. I don't know much North American poetry that fits the category, but there are traces in the music you hear on the radio. My friend Deben Bhattacharya, who died a few years ago, conscientiously translated a good deal of *ninda stuti* in his books on the Bauls of Bengal and their unconventional mystical poetry. Here, in the American West, in a less conscious, more conspicuous way, *ninda stuti* has been done piecemeal for two hundred years by the mountain men, immigrants, military surveys, and traders who entered the Rocky Mountain bioregion where I live.

Walt Whitman wrote, "the United States themselves are the greatest poem." Once you realize how weird, ironic, and humorously deprecating the place names of the American West are, you start to hear the landscape itself as a song of twisty, abusively phrased devotion. Hell's Half Acre, Devil's Postpile, High Lonesome. Quandary Peak; Blue Sky Basin (the current name for Category III).

Once, in search of a Rocky Mountain lyric, I compiled a list poem made up of nearby place-names with my daughter Althea. We used a Colorado atlas full of topographical maps and a gazette. Here's what we came up with, our *ninda stuti*, laughing & rolling about as we sang—

A town called Elizabeth.
A town called Gothic.
A town called Troublesome.
A canyon called Chaos.
A rock called Elk Tooth.
A town called McCoy.
A gulch called Skeleton.
A town called Boone.
A town called Goodnight.
A creek called Horse.
A pass called Pawnee.
A lake called Chipmunk.
A creek called Squeak.
A park called Interlocken.
A town called Paradox.
A peak called Quandary.
A town called Rifle.
A rock called Bishop's Prick.
A peak called Thunderbolt.
A mine called Buckskin.
A town called River Bend.
A bar called Rocky Flats.

Arrangement by Althea & Andrew Schelling. Original composition by dozens of ornery, one-word-poem settlers.

The *Two Elk* entries come from three sequential notebooks. When I begin a notebook I make a vermilion imprint on the flyleaf with a Chinese soapstone *chop* or signature-seal. I number the pages and establish a few at the back for an index. The notebook eventually acquires a name—a name, I like to call it, not a title— drawn from a central image or phrase that shows up. The first of the autumn notebooks is called *Reflection*, the second *Two Elk*. The third is just a distant bark in the mountains.

Andrew Schelling
December 2003 / June 2005
Southern Rocky Mountain Ecosystem

Two Elk

thoughts written down thus in a journal might be printed in the same form with greater advantage—than if the related ones were brought together in separate essays. They are now allied to life—& are seen by the reader not far fetched—It is more simple—less artful.

H.D. Thoreau

... I set about filling the notebooks with odd facts, stories from the past, and all sorts of other things, often including the most trivial material. On the whole I concentrated on things and people that I found charming and pleasant; my notes are also full of poems and observations on trees and plants, birds and insects. I was sure that when people saw my book they would say, "It's even worse than I expected...."

Sei Shonagon

16 August 2003

Dorothy Lake, an hour & a half above Fourth of July mine.
Quick swim at 12,000 feet—ragged escarpments, snowfield rotting into
the northside water. Ate a hasty sandwich. A thunder god growled off the rocks,
then penetrating wind.
Cold hands hard to write—

The first dry pellets of rain arrive
as I trace the Divide by foot
        out of nowhere clouds congealing—
        was clear sky now abruptly I'm walking
        in wind-driven icy cloud
hail breaks out in earnest, thunder
retorts off the pinnacles,
& my hair bristles at streak lightning, sizzling rain

        "Edited by cold & hunger, revised by hunger & cold."

These days the poems come mostly in lines. Have haibun days been forgot?
When the writing always appeared in blocks of prose—?
Descend a thousand feet & brew tea under a twisted limber pine.
You'd never know it had stormed. Massive white volumetric clouds of the S. Rockies
—docked overhead, piled soft in the heights—gandharva palaces
& ridges that fall to far-away cities.
The American challenge was: reinvent the poetic line. Behind that, or before—
a love for vernacular, to locate our own speech. Cloud messenger
scraping the lichen.
Meghaduta.

          *   *

Girls with wild hair
        go past in pickups—
note: saddle-soap hiking boots, get new laces
If there be gods, up here you find them
        far-out skywalker ladies, pacing the thunderstruck ridge

17 August

Up high is "god realm"
        not Buddhist deva delight & sensual frolic world
—tundra realm instead, & humans visit with caution—
ice carved rock, tiny wind-stunted pine, clanging ridges, snarls of lightning
reporting along broken crests; vast ice sheets, cliffs coming apart as you watch, storms
from nowhere. Rough winds through the mountain aperture seize your breath,
& lichen & small bright moss—

           for fur-less human a tough place
even summer months
          good for pilgrim visit or cautious excursion
a few hours, days, near to the gods
              then scamper down home—

18 August

     "The naturalist's trance was adaptive: the glimpse of one small
     animal hidden in the grass could make a difference…"
                    E.O. Wilson

A notebook without a dream?

Lama Govinda thought meditation began among hunters in the Himalaya foothills

col : the pass between two peaks,
          gap in a ridge

talus : debris of rock, sloping at cliff base

20 August

M in her bedroom, what were her words? "They all fit."
The dresser beyond her olive-color bedclothes & thick arabesque quilt—
she's folding articles of clothing into drawers & cubicles—
light wood, maple or Oriental with black ring-handles, sizable, pressing
it all in. "They fit," is what she says. Bedroom door where windows
should be. Then strides over to the portal with an almost
leer, stretching her arms across the frame—both eyes on me—
face a dog Dakini face

> snout canine, smiling almost benign
> her red-blond hair

22 August

Mars—in the east at 9:00 p.m.—close to Earth as it ever gets—
34,646,418 miles distant. 59,619 years ago the last time orbit brought it this near.
Neanderthal had 30 thousand years left. No cave art. A few centuries hence, will creep
even closer. From Sanitas Valley, a steady red-amber beacon, above the stark, black-
gnarl'd pines of Dakota Ridge.

> "...& they every one in their bright loins
> Have a beautiful golden gate that opens into the vegetative world"
> Wm. Blake

24 August

The raw facts of human existence, shall we name them? Solitude, loneliness, fear.
The unmixed emotions rise up, & are powers, call'd into presence—
anger & fear, bewilderment, loathing & guilt. Take refuge in the small
mosses at 12,000 feet. Moss campion, petals the color of
intimate flesh—

low, out of the wind,
bruise a leaf it smells pungent, crouched open for
pleasure

29 August

Ravens toss over the windy jagged pinnacles
scraps of night sky
multidimensional pathways: snake love, serpentine energy syntax
devious kisses, us ophidian, crawl around in a tangle—
        that's how we make it

& Ursa Major points the way north—
notebook for tundra poetics /
lost on the twisty pathways of love /
what makes us human /
        gray fox I thought, she said it's cougar—

        she was right,
a small mammal hung from its mouth

1 September

Wasps in the garden come & go. The acorn squash beneath its broad leaf.
Broccoli, kale, chard, zuccini. Faraway peaks nearly empty of snow.
One early black cap chickadee, 6:00 a.m. its two-note song.
Now after a decade I discover my problem with the stove, its guttering
weak initial flame is caused by overfilling the tank. I'd forgotten to
refill it before thundergod tea, the flame leaps to alertness, and "the obligation
of a dream was as binding as a vow…." Over our sweet bed, "disregard
        of either was said to be punished by the forces
        of nature."
        (Frances Densmore, *Music of the Teton Sioux*)

5 September

And in the before-dawn glow from the east
a repeated cry scrapes the flank of Mt. Sanitas—
        feline?   mountain lion?
finally I rose from bed, went to the casement

studied the mountain
saw sky reddening but no longer heard the bluesy
lonesome cry—

felis concolor : puma

Sp. from Quechua, *puma*

…and there'd been an impoverished elderly Tibetan lady, two small daughters,
trying to sell the saddest trashy items—all that's left when I arrive are two
screwdrivers. One has a red plastic handle & down its blade engraved Chinese
lettering, the other yellow plastic with English words. Her tiny
daughters keep trying to peer into my wallet. I have several single dollars and one
two-dollar bill. I want the red-handled Chinese one but the crone is adamant—
I must take the yellow—

cougar: cognate to jaguar

both from Tupi Indian: "deer-colored"

"thy stiff-drying deer-colored pelt"
How'd I discover that line for a poem, before seeing
the dictionary?

6 September

"In the heart it's *chih* (life-force), in language
it's *shih* (poetry)."

I got this from Red Pine.

A poem has nothing to fear from the scholars, they can't hurt it. They can't
block its *shakti,* its coil'd power. Neither can you. The left part of the ideogram
stands for "language," the right "from the heart." In Tu Fu's *shih*
the Yangtze watershed indicates:

hermits, bandits, exiled officials, lost poets.

Wednesday the harvest moon. September's good for looking at Mars.

7 September

McClure tells me he has "twenty-six shelf feet" of journals in a room at
the Bancroft. For the first time I hear the crack of age in his voice.
Crickets loud & urgent at night. Autumn is cricket death—they feel it.
M. fed me lamb stew with zuccini & herbs from her garden. I found with
surprise in a notebook, as though it had not been mine, this recent dream: suburban
bungalow outfitted with filthy orange shag carpet—cheap consumer trash
tossed in the corners—then my hair bristles! Tiger pawprints matted into the rug. Also
strips of flesh & crack'd bone—droppt from its
jaws
overnight—

11 September

Weird to catch myself brooding—two & a half years later—
over destruction of the Bamiyan buddhas.
Bow to the piles of rubble under our own nearby peaks; they too
are bones of the old-time buddhas.

In Longmont Julie Seiko's elderly neighbors tell her six weeks
after cricket song comes the year's first frost. "Kingfisher sleeves."
Pick tomatoes before second frost—that one will
kill them. Our old people still carry agriculture lore the young never learnt.
And Lucien, eighty-seven, tells very simply of Normandy:
"I got blown up in a ditch. They carried me back on a stretcher."
Years later meets a German soldier who'd stood opposite that day—Panzer corps—
& becomes tight friends. Now, both late eighties, they meet once more to visit
the European memorials & say final good-byes. Of fifty thousand lyrics
in *Complete Poems of the T'ang Dynasty*
                only one was composed by a Buddhist nun—

> Troubled thoughts come to the traveler
> An old fisherman gets spooked by his dreams—
> This wobbly boat
>   followed by a wobbly moon
> Unbroken mountains bending south & north
>   (Haijin)

How do I know "south & north" mountains? Ours stretch to Wyoming—is
answer enough. That way the Medicine Bows. It all occurs in the detail.
Note to include dream data in natural history notebook. I learnt this from ancient
Chinese; also Teton Sioux, (Frances Densmore's ethnographic report).
Language of the dream body is language
of the waken'd body, just a bit looser, or darker. Instead of moon viewing last night
(cloud cover too thick) M. & I broke cottonwood branches apart—
Monday's storm had scattered about—
        to bed & made harvest moon love.

12 September

Today I got a feverish astral San Francisco vision: the Barbary Coast—
Scotch sailors, perfumed whores, Nob Hill dowagers, dotty countess from Scottish
highland parish, a ghost dead from knife, waifish girls who hunger for lovers, gun-
toting reformers, gamblers, staggering drunks: Helen Adam's opera. Now someone
should write it for Denver. The house of Mattie Silk—mirror wall whorehouse,
its mistress dead in a hotel room shot once through the temple—
By 1943 my WPA Guide denotes it a Buddhist temple—

        "the only one between
                San Francisco & New York"
                limestone building unusual in Denver a
                city where brick predominates

First snow on the foothills, down to 6000'. Clear day here, high peaks are
cloud hid.

13 September

Two dark blue channels of energy, one originating in each testicle,
coiling up to my nipples. From my mouth a limp fox corpse, freshly dead, its fur
dust-blue. When we awoke, talked tenderly—the fear of how exposing one's
inward life incites jealousy—it's fifty degrees out—. And sexual intimacy? best access
to shaman spheres? Clanging peaks overhead, one route to self-knowledge:
soft barks of ecstasy another—

That blue-green calm behind the eyes.

14 September

A dark room. Waking I see my "husband," slightly apologetic,
a small, anguished looking Chinese man in soft herringbone suit. He twists a
worn gray fedora in his hands, pulling a chair to the end of my bed. Above him
apparition—another frame—looks like a sage smudge with stick of wet black
opium, gold Chinese letters incised down its length.
"Our daughters," selecting his words carefully—
he's traced their problems to my addiction. Sitting up I see red-golden gleam
of two moxa cones he's placed on my shins. Going to heal me…

Dream gender shift—?
due to yesterday reading in *Vimalakirti Sutra*? No, dream's too close to the bone.
I harvested a sackful of chard, some stray kale leaves, & tiny season end
broccoli crowns. Days drawing short.

15 September

2:00 pm left car at Flagstaff, bushwhacked up a north slope to view of
the high peaks. Cloudless day, a band of smog across Front Range cities so
the eye fails before Kansas. Caught Ranger Trail a short distance, then left
it for tempting cliffside ascent—sandwiched red sandstone & composite layers—
to a farther ridge. Leaping boulder to boulder, not " glacial erratics" but
errantly tossed down the summit.

At one point tested present-moment awareness shimmying up a jamcrack, feet
hanging over the canyon. At the top Okemo rewards me with that dog-face—
half puzzled half patronizing: you could have gone
around.

Has anyone figured why Doug fir cones hang down?
                    that little three-fork tongue
            & bract openings of precise shape & dimension so
                        only *its* pollen can enter
        like giving a housekey to your lover
all this to say vertigo is fear of
                    down & back
            heights & flesh-fuck ecstasies

"Your addiction" sd/ Marlow after I
recounted the dream
        & momentarily I got perturbed out of guilt—

                *   *

Wang Wei heard axe sound
& knew he wasn't alone on the mountain
far-off
motorcycle gears do
      it for this poet you're
      never alone on a mountain

End Green Mtn. entry // 3:50 pm

    (not Gore Range, that there's Mt. Bancroft)

17 September

Day begins early—it's a downhill slope eastward to Kansas
Sun contracting with the equinox—
        bright cold haze over Oz
        collar of clouds over our western paradise peaks
Declining days of summer, good for treating the earth element says Jim
setting the bright needles to stomach & spleen meridians,
same points as the Chinese man in Sunday night's dream

On the young, a dragon realm of tattoos & piercings. Eruption of the primitive into
contemporary culture? Or absorption by the market of the body's surface? When
the market corrects itself again, and we in Colorado lose "power" (natural gas costs
rising 73% this winter says Xcel),
the real power lines will be what we clutch'd
                  coming into this world
          hormonal instinct & compass point wisdom
                        the only poems publish't will come off the handpress

18 September

Shaft of sunlight
turns the tea amber—
        late summer green enamel unicorn cup

20 September

Colorado's characteristic red sandstone forms the high altitude mountain bowl I'm rambling through. The slopes are covered with rotten, unstable snow. Suddenly I hear it— a low rumble— & notice some first few pebbles starting dangerously down. Quickly I ferret about for shelter from avalanche—& locate protective boulder, size of a car, with cup-like hollow in its underside. Althea's above though—I'm pleading she join me. No—she wants—disoriented by peril—to remain & die with friends.

Behind is a massive dormitory, people pressed against windowpanes, gesturing franticly. I smell the wall of snow coming. In an instant the building will explode—

so catch Althea in my arms & cradle her—just as I did the night she was born, tiny, shaking with hormones & instinct under the wax-like moon—& draw her into the hollow. When the avalanche hits, our boulder lofts to the surface & travels slowly along the sea of churning snow. Safely we study the high country as we pass, its striated pinnacles & angular buttresses. Can I read the geology? Much debris churns upwards from the snow—boots, hats, cups, sweaters—detritus of civilization. The crushed building.

The Teton Sioux spoke of it—
how the dream visits you with responsibility. Dream, if it comes from the thunderbirds, more binding than a vow.

Last November, standing in icy gusts at Blue Lake with Marlow, I saw the natural world provide the same image as the I Ching we'd tossed. Again & again in the months that followed, the same message if I looked close. Good counsel is provided by the seasonal elements, if you study nature with open eye. The dream too—last night's unfolding the hexagram I'd gotten the day before. *Retire*. It even articulated the changing lines.

24 September

In the mail Jane Hirshfield sends a Bodhidharma poem. Uncharacteristic humor for her. Some Zen master's seeking work at MacDonald's. Then there's the story of Kobun Chino that M. told me—

How the Zen Master Got through Airport Security

"Did you pack your own bags?"

No.

"Have your bags been under your control?"

No.

Surely it is a problem of translation. The agent produces a laminated card with two dozen scripts. "Which language do you understand the question in?" He studies the card with great concentration before looking up.

All of them.

*　　　*

9:00 pm

Red fox on the street when I step from the house.
He studies me a moment, then turns & slips through a gap in
Tim & Leni's fence—

down the street one doe & one fawn
a hundred yards farther one doe & two fawn
The animal powers still visit.
Sure hope rangers don't shoot that bear sow
on Sanitas.

27 September

The poison ivy has flagged. Bitter leaf-work gone skeletal.
Miner who built cabin in crotch of Shadow Canyon must've been crazy,
cooped up all winter with a mind of ice. The book
on my lap is heavy it says—

> a fancy for a certain animal
> preceded a dream
> > concerning it

"The animals want to communicate with man, but Wakan'tanka does not
intend that they shall do so directly—man must do the greater part in
securing an understanding."

And how does one proceed? "Let a man decide upon his animal, and make a study
of it. Let him learn to understand its sounds and motions."

Two weeks ago Johnny Cash. Wednesday Edward Said. Now George Plimpton.
Days I don't read the *Times* who is it?

Poem

No butter at home, no flour. A long oblong pan slips off the shelf.
Is this how the T'ang Dynasty fell?
"Morning fog in the southern gorge"
& all their brushwork with it
Someone baked a Brown Betty
from apples picked on Apple Valley Road—
This is a prayer that Althea
not get caught, smoking weed—

28 September

DEATH OF KALIDASA

      end of Edward Said

Is Althea telling me about friends getting busted to elicit sympathy?
Or prepare me for crisis? Uh-oh.

                poison on Kalidasa to steal his poem

    amber   ruby   asafetida   turmeric

        Western meadowlark bring me to my senses
cows have trod the low meadow
        Brake for Moose
        It Might Save Your Life

29 September

Mt. Audubon

    Left car 9:25 Mitchell Lake trailhead. The long northward traverse across
Audubon's broad, grassy, east-facing slope. The square summit of Long's Peak sets
a clear northerly beacon—where John Wesley Powell made first documented climb
one hundred thirty-four years ago. Today the plains an ocean of haze. Out there lies
Kansas.

    Why does Oz of my daughter's childhood & my own—books—come to
mind when the eye drifts toward Boot Hill? Is it high altitude that furls back the
membrane between perception & childhood delight? I'm at upper limit of the
krumholz. A few east-leaning spruce growths; willow brush lies crimson in their
dark leeward shadow where some refuge is had from the wind. As always a stiff
wind comes dropping across the Divide—

    Last time up here, four Novembers ago with Tom Morgan. Slopes
covered that day with ice. Somewhere below the summit my thumbs went funny
and couldn't work the zipper of the jacket. Why'd I stay up late drinking scotch?

Numb with cold, unable to fit the icy water bottle to my lips, short on food, breath in irregular gasps; & now the *dakinis* were taking me. Hands swollen from mountain edema; windy song luring me toward that fatal glacier-cut cirque. Tom pinned me with his naturalist's eye, studied my reflex, & judged me okay for final push to the summit. If you're in trouble your pupils dilate even in sun. Mountain know-how, solid as basalt: & up we went—

At the summit Tom let me go. I flopped into largest of four stone semi-circle shelters in a half dream. *Dakinis* are skywalker girls. One spread her legs over my mouth & took the oxygen. Salt, hormones, blood, a haze of mineral, crisp taste of metal on the tongue. The only sense remaining was taste. I couldn't see or hear. My first thought was it tasted like woman—the spooky meat on the tongue—then got thrown farther back—unable to explain but suddenly knew: *taste of myself.* And for a moment lost consciousness.

When we got back to town I wrote it up in a poem. That the mountain had taught taste as the primal sense, the perception born where the planet gets born, high among rock. The Hindu poets once taught it also—

> somewhere rock gives off
> its hollow echo-retort
> across the ravine San Isabelle Glacier

—*taste*, the one perception in which you take the object into your body. So the question arises, how close can you get to emotion? In the poem, India, they went for *rasa*: the taste of purest emotion. Call it bedrock. "The Self is *rasa*," said Abhinavagupta in Kashmir—"the Self of poetry." Him also a high altitude traveler.

So Judith's book on dream-stalker vision ladies is *The Dakini's Warm Breath*. Note to ask her about lore in Tibet: what do they tell of *dakinis* & high altitude consciousness? Two raven wheel from the peak, catching a swift spiral updraft. They see things this human eye cannot. Tom saw *her* in my eye & knew I was close. "Stay north. The cliffs are to the south." There is no language for these rocks, torn to rubble by glacier, scaled by pounding winter, patterned with florets of black lichen, barked with knobs & protuberances.

A sharp gust would take you 2000 feet over the precipice to Coney Lake. Forget the *dakini's* warm breath—what of fatal ice goddess nipples? Mere lack of judgment?

tea & salted almonds at 13,322 feet

2 October

Today I start a new notebook, now what to name it?
Blue floral Japanese paper
frail tendril blossoms of silver adorn the cover.
Chill overcast morning. What
        contrast to Monday's climb into Audubon sunsplash.

5 October

Calligraphy & poetry as two arts divided by only a thin membrane: the Orient.

One enormous yellowing cottonwood leaf
falls into the Japanese maple that
        shelters Kuan-yin
      maroon, olive, copper: mottled fall foliage

should I take Mt. Audubon entry & shape a dakini poem,
           —part of ongoing Buddhist scripture scroll?

6 October   *Hessie Townsite Trailhead*

      In the direction of Devil's Thumb, alongside Jasper Creek (got its name from the map), M. & myself rise into an open grassy swale. Far on can see the Divide & the gnarled upcrop of granite someone thought a massive wart-covered thumb. Diabolical place names of the American West. Wonder if anyone's gathered a list? Patches of snow on talus slopes. By 10,000 feet the aspen leaves mostly gone. In the rocks below, the braids of water are singing. Jasper the stone or some miner's name?

      We ditched the heavy tea-making supplies off-trail under a diminutive fir, marking the site. "If I can't remember where the tea-kit's hidden I have no business in mountains." Always study the landscape, someone taught me—may need to know it for a future life.

      4:00 pm retrieved cached supplies
      Did I set out with too little fuel in the stove? It has gone out quite

unexpectedly & will not re-light. Quick high altitude dream what. Kissing her belly. Visible answer dragon. Stroke her tummy & together drift on whose "orchid boat." Chinese euphemism. And the water, did it get hot enough for dragon tea?

> One occluded aspen leaf
> gives echo to schist—
> wherever we sit

…while here water coils through tough archaic granite & the world seems fresh. Settling comfortably into sheets of rock, think I'll sit here a thousand years or so— rain, snow, sun, wind, season me, weather this body, sculpt it in dawnlight. I'll come out shapeshifted, & see what people look like ten thousand years, over those hills. More in love? less prone to confusion? Wonder what kind poems they write. New emotions discover? Unprecedented positions for love? Nah—

> This creature rock & ice
> an autumn insect,
> gone before the dogtooth violet falls

7 October

At dusk harvested several sacks of chard, kale, squash, broccoli, & herbs from the garden with M. I sippt red wine & listened to the ballgame—Red Sox defeating the A's—she made squash soup. Dream my car is stolen. A student. Trouble for drugs or money.
I have to force the keys from him.

8 October

> *Why quarrel with our bliss?*
> then a slightly obscure line that ends
> *kiss—*
> face youthful & amber by candlelight
> "Between the desire & the spasm…"
> this
> this
> *this*

9 October

Lista for Mountain Tea Ceremony

Stove. Black tea is best for the high country. Tea-kettle, a Japanese tetsubin of cast iron though heavy works well. Tea-strainer. Spoon. Enamel camping cups, or thick ceramic cups wrapped in cloth if your expectation is formal. Fresh matches. Extra stove fuel. It is terrible to run out of fuel in the mountains. You have to explain to companions that you are generally better prepared, and if it is cold everyone though trying to be polite will look out of sorts. An embroidered towel or napkin. Milk. Sugar.
Dragon cookies.

I sat in the meadow beneath Devil's Thumb
             watching the wind roll across
                      this planet.
         I saw rock scale & erode, watched whole forests seep
back into soil.
                      airliners creased the sky & at night satellites
             Mars drew close then retreated
                      the Western Barbarian tangled thoughts with my own
         We are carbon, magnesium, sodium, wrangled into
                               five elements
                      held in one precious Mind.
             When all that remained was a sunbleached
                      ribcage, a few crack'd bones, & two empty
                               skull sockets
         I rose & returned to the city—

The aspen are flares of cadmium, cinnabar, chartreuse, & apricot.
Brows of sedimentary rock.

All I ask,
who can make friends with lichen?

9 October

... returning to my seat at the bar with tiny gold flask of Guinness I gaze out the sizable windows onto a rushing creek. Sweeping downstream over the rocks suddenly come life-size Dia des Muertos skeletal figures, white bones & colorful sombreros slipping past quickly. Flood? is it flash flood up valley—? At the bar people seem edgy, the sky darkens. An automobile tumbles past on the water, then another, a square 60s Rambler. It lodges nose down before the window. Someone reaches to open its door & I see the booted leg of a woman flop hopelessly from the rear seat. I refuse to join this—refuse to partake in the plunder—can't sit & wait for catastrophe—debris of civilization tossing violently past I want no part of—
       & light off for higher ground—

only to waken pestered by the lyric:

       Here I sit / all alone with a broken heart
       Took three bennies / and my semi-truck won't start

Rock found in the Northern & Southern Rocky Mountain zones:

          rhyolite
          basalt
          granite
          sandstone
          travertine
          limestone
          gneiss
          schist

Feeling unutterably close to M these days
          her face unexpectedly sweet in candle glint
       of the dearest hands, of the smoky voice

10 October

Special is the blue-dark of a sky appearing along the west ridge near dawn. Just as evening holds a particular quality of light to the sky, the hour before sunrise holds a particular quality of *dark*. West Nile virus brought terrible damage, Jenny Heath tells me, to local bird populations, particularly corvids. That magpie flopping in the alley September—not leg broken but West Nile infected?—to die alone alongside neighbor's drainpipe.

> ...concealed, button-like, how little known, now a shy wild creature, button-like in the red tangle of hair. I want to know this person, fold her in safety & delight. How does a person endure, how can anyone stand it, with a consort—without a consort—to open the sweet golden gates?

*   *

Perhaps it is the season, late summer—
>as though trees were too slow I have
>fallen in love with rock:
>>tectonic movement not far from the compression power of
>>dream: igneous: "extrusive"

>*formed as lava erupts explosively*
>>this is rhyolite, the one rock type not recognized by spell-check

Nor can locate in any Sanskrit dictionary *dakini*. The word surviving in Tibetan only?

>"at or near the earth's surface, or oozes
>out of the ground more slowly"

Each time, the summits of Indian Peaks give the same instruction: the gods are made cheerful by craft.

11 October

Yesterday we established the poetry tree. Discarded rice paper calligraphy cut into strips, out in the autumn calligraphy garden. Visitors write poems & affix them to the soft dominant pine by the studio door with scarlet yarn. "Like prayer flags," giggles Binky over the telephone. Wind produces a great flapping sound, the poems carry across the planet, the articulations & durations produce rhythmic pleasures & insight: may they bring solace to living creatures....

For love is full of sinewy windings. Notebook keeps falling open, page 7, where it ardently inquires about troubled seasons of love; yet here, eleven pages deeper I muse on how rich & gratifying it's become, as though independent of our efforts or calibrated to seasons no human can quite find in the almanac. Last night I whispered: how splendid, calligraphy, paintings, the pride I take in your gestures & speech, the toss of hair—as we made love. Autumn's wistful harvest pleasures. Time now to bring them home. Hunter's moon tenebrous unclouded sky inside our saddening hearts.

> Gusts of wind
> hot sun & cool air contest like dragons
> around the poetry tree—

And here where the Great Plains end in the rainshadow, and the Devil's Backbone opens its rough gap to the mountains, we take wind as others take rain. Listen, it carries solace, deep in the year, deep in night. Even icy banshee howls of dark solstice, grating along the corners of the house bring a surge of comfort. How blessed to lie here, "pumpkin vines wrapped over the cottage's / little thatch roof," wrapt up close by her breasts.

> Now I must tell of the magic bird script
> of the Taoist sorcerers—
> how one watches the talismans
> twist into birds
> soon they wind thew-like about & lift
> from the jade green page

Maya, age seven. On the tree her poem says

> My love
> My peace
> My fun
> My song

31

14 October

A poem situated in the Indian Peaks wilderness. To soothe
the wounded heart—

<u>Dakini</u> is spellt
with a palatal *d* (*murdhanya*) not dental (*danta*)
hence find it now in Monier-Williams dictionary
fr. *Daka*, an imp attendant on Kali
(in the *Kalachakra*)
Dakini, female imp
feeding on human flesh

Go first to dreams for counsel, royal switchback into the unconscious. Then to *I Ching*. When these prove inscrutable, resort to bumper stickers—or fragment of song off the radio. *Oracles appear everywhere*, my lady love hath shown me. Tune the car stereo & hear a rustle of yarrow stalks. Even a poem might come through.

> "For a deity with chthonian associations Hermes has very little to
> do with divination and oracles."
> *The Oxford Classical Dictionary*

Patron of poets patron of thieves. If the car radio delivers a line for your poem, is that theft? Hermes has little to do with oracles, I have gotten only a few lines of poetry off the car radio, yet at Pharae there existed a small temple according to my reference book—

> "Here the consultant, after paying his respects to the god, stopped
> his ears till he got beyond the market-place where the temple stood;
> the first words he heard when he unstopped them were the answer
> to any question he had asked of Hermes."

> The most searing
> pain of all
> to bring anguish on those
> you love

18 October

And as for understanding how languages alter, written records do drop into a fairly distant past, perhaps 5000 years... writing however is but one tiny plot in riotous landscapes of oral speech. Or a series of gardens tended in neat little rows within vast untamable ecosystems. Simplistic to think that by scouring libraries (troves of accumulated writings) one could discern the forces that make language change. As well explain the succession of forest trees by studying how corn got cultivated—harvest & hybridize—

> "...in language we inherit the voices of the dead. Language is
> passed on to us by people who are now in their graves and brings
> with it access to history, tradition, times and places that are not at
> all immediate to our own... particular occasion."
>
> Nathaniel Mackey

It begins outside. Into it we come, as into biology or culture. At the end vanish from it. Very little we do can bring any change. It is a vast ecosystem, beyond our comprehension, & very conservative in its structure. It shifts according to forces we cannot see or predict. How long have we tracked its changes? Not long enough to see it shapeshift.

> Old as ice
> scraping these thoughts with glacial firmness—
> *voice*

> Vedic goddess Vak, to whom a few old prayers
are still due—

19 October

8:00 a.m. loaded packs into Tim Hogan's truck. Drove through Lyons, turned south, & parked at St. Vrain Mountain trailhead amid a scatter of rural cottages. Ascended 3100 feet in stiff wind, Wild Basin dropping off northward. Beyond, can observe Mt. Meeker, Long's Peak, Pagoda Peak, Chief's Head, & Mt. Alice (listing them north to south). The Rockies older than the Sierra Nevada, Tim says. Last glaciation—the Wisconsin—claws of ice worked over the already existent rock forms:

gneiss, schist, & granite. This is why above tree-line the Sierras are smooth, bare rock. The Rockies in contrast have accumulated soil—even here, 12,162 feet—laid across older formations. Silt & debris deposited by wind—why does it bring to mind the weather exposed skeleton of Basho? Into this soil bed arrive seeds, insects, and the start of whole ecosystems. Delicate flora, ancient kin in the evolutionary line.

St. Vrain: the creek originally named Potera's

> "…from a Frenchman of that name who is said to have been
> bewildered upon it, wandering about for 20 days almost without
> food. He was found by a band of Kiowas, who frequent this part
> of the country, and restored to his companions, a party of hunters
> at that time encamped on the Arkansas."

Creek, glaciers, and peak later named for the brothers St. Vrain who set up a trading post on the Platte River, mile and a half below where the creek enters. They traded sugar and looking glasses for buffalo hide. Sioux, Cheyenne, Shoshoni, Pawnee, Apache, came through.

> (Fifth anniversary Vail ski resort fire, Category III.)

> *If you build it we will burn it. The ELFs are angry.*

Notes:

* Ten million or more species still alive on the planet.

* Biodiversity the most information-rich part of the known universe.
    (Despite living organisms comprising only one ten-billionth of earth's mass.)

* "We arose from other organisms already here."

* "Fucking thermos won't keep the tea for three hours—"
    like a Chevrolet, it's American.

21 October

The yoga of dreamcatching has begun to falter.
Hybrid, sex indeterminate, a mass of
reddish hair.
The vocables "zam" / or "sama."

24 October

Two Elk Trail, just out of Minturn. Start by the shooting range.
7 1/2 miles up creek to the pass. We've walked three miles, eat a sandwich just
across a low wooded pass from Vail's incursion into Category III. A ski trail leads
up there. Marlow wears the blaze orange vest we found carefully folded under a
branch by the trail. When we queried a hunter on his cell phone he advised, "wear
orange." Funny, I wrote about this place last week.

       If you build it we will burn it. The ELFs are angry.

Gone in the night in petroleum blaze: two lifts & a restaurant.
I must write about the sea mammal tooth I wear on rawhide about my neck. But
near this thicket that smells of recent bear was last reported sighting of a lynx in
Colorado. "In the shadows there / may be a lynx or there / may not"

          no native cat seen
             since '73

6:00 p.m.
A number of animalitos, tiny bright Michoacan animals of some light-weight wood:
el tigre, a fantastic duck creature, coyote, black jaguar with a curled crimson mouth.
They begin to drop from the bed to the floor. Several break. The others mill about in
confusion. It's up to me to repair them with glue...
restore them to life...

25 October

> "In India women are viewed as more libidinous than men, making demands upon them that cannot be satisfied. When refused, popular Indian culture suggests, some women might become witches (in Hindi, *dakan* or *dahani*) who would exact their revenge by feasting on the blood of their decapitated male adversary."
>
> Judith Simmer-Brown

Took Castle Creek Road to Conundrum Creek trailhead. A small array of vehicles parked at the valley mouth. Mostly hunters. A dormitory tent, white canvas, with a 55 gallon drum cut into a stove. Coolers & camouflage gear. Camouflage? with blaze orange over it?

"We gonna get shot if we go up that creek—?"

"I wouldn't shoot you," looking me over closely, "you don't have big enough horns."

> childhood attention to
> body parts:
> *the butchering perception*

26 October

How interesting that dakinis suck *rasa* (spirit juice) out of a man for revenge. Do not let them near the poem—the poem too is diffused with *rasa*. Thus sayeth Abhinavagupta of Kashmir many centuries ago. In the dream a woman thrusts her hands into wet leaf mold at the root of a tree, searching for jewelry.

Long live the Earth Liberation Front.

27 October

"The dead end of remaking the gods in human form."

          … *raudra* : the rasa of fury
               —did Jessica mean this by darkness—
                   "let in some darkness" or

"…beware the fury of a patient man."

A virulent growl crawls into the throat—the wreckage of wild habitat—wrath over dull-witted greed, the cramping of humor, the techno- bewilderment; oh Furies we've come to a pass where humans gnaw their own asphalt hearts, & set up their children on pavement—

          The rural hunter with his hi-tech carbine, tripod slung on the shoulder, camouflage rifle scope, dirty new pickup, orange vest, down mittens, rugged boots, & global positioning system, shows a consideration for tool & artifact deficient in most urban dwellers.

"The gods are made cheerful by craft."

          One sharpens one's knife, changes oil in one's car, greases one's boots, orders one's manuscripts. Then to lay one's books carefully away on the shelf. Does punctuation work the same way? A care for how objects get made—

        Witless haiku
     script me no ice-bound miner's shack—
          October willow

         *   *

Cathedral Lake   (11,862')

This creature's more fully at home, at 12,000'
             than anywhere else—

The pinnacles soar. Spires, domes, escarpments, buttresses: give them names from a book of architecture. Above the restless black water. Dark-violet wind-scoured sandstone, pale caramel, dusty gray purple, seams of charcoal, flint-green strata, burnt chocolate shale.

Follow the ridge to Electric Pass—13,500'—highest pass with a name in Colorado. Up there dreams wait the traveler. I came through alone; hungry ghosts beat on my skull all night; in the morning cold granola. Here, below the cathedrals—bent to a notebook, ink sluggish from cold—wind sends a froth over the lake—fingers balled with the chill, more animal paw than a hand. Weather shifting, a steely sun drops behind the far sawtooth.

> Edited by frost
>> scaled by first snow

Temples? cathedrals? groves of intricate bio-mass? high rock precipices? Where dakinis, those queer little rust-color florets of lichen, & other semi-divines hang out? (Plants have adapted to extreme conditions of wind, ice, unsheathed sun, scant moisture.) This fragile high altitude world. In India—says Madhav Gadgil— reverence for nature slowly coerced into a reverence for artifact—

> the word *gadget*, what is its origin, Gadgil?

On the S. Asian subcontinent, your essays tell us, holy groves go into timber, the forests harvested & replaced by swank temples. (Our bioregion, it is subdivisions & business parks named for what they replace.) This primate with a love for gadgetry, for artifact. And then a collusion of Brahmans: the sacred groves stripped & toppled; garish cathedrals of stone, mortar, plaster, & bright corrugated iron go up in their stead. The Brahmans, who recite at dawn the *gayatri* hymn, get kickbacks from timber foremen by dusk—

> A story to spur rage—
> may it bring out the ELF
>> Earth Liberation Front

The cobalt watery surface now flitting with ripples it's time
>> to descend or get caught—
>> can I warm my hands on your breasts?

your breasts like the eyes that I see with dear Marlow?
                              Twilight, scent of snow driven down from the north
                              fast-moving horse-tail clouds—

In the south, Cathedral Peak's 13,943

                              Conundrum's 14,022

Did I name the notebook Two Elk or Two Elf?

30 October

Broke the forest green teapot this morning, comrade of years. Three realms, three
houses, three hundred roads. A guide through rough psychic terrain; protection
from sorcery; outlasted a marriage; solace in winter; gadget for long hours of
writing.

Now we know: excursion to Cathedral Lake was final
high country
            trip of the season—
Gadget: "origin unknown"

Replace teapot.
Embrace "high country art."

3 November

        Fox ghost? First a confounding number of roadkill. I'd seen skunk,
raccoon, many squirrel, some kind of dog, & several deer. Each left a bloody tire-
track and scattered fur. On this stretch of road though, the nothing's spookier. We'd
turned onto Hickory Ridge. An SUV came over the hill, slowed, and extinguished
its headlights—

        —then it sprang from the bushes—fox? dog? feral cat?—and went under
the hood. Crushing the brake I shuddered & knew it was dead. But Althea and
Henry saw nothing. We backed down the road to study the asphalt by headlight. No
trace. Lights of a farm in the distance. Something whimpered—but the sound came
across the pasture to us. Fox ghost? Caught in an onslaught of guilt I dug out this
poem from *Devil's Thumb Notebook* when I got home—

Untitled

Followed a red fox
over the hill

wonder what girl she was
dressed up funny in a bushy tail

thoughts like that just get yourself trouble

grey splintered fence
grass in the ruined floorboards
what could I do it was so

long ago

4 November

Your pleasure is of more interest to me than my own.

Historic places known to classical poetry are *uta-makura*, poetry places [Japan]. Places "discovered" by haikai poets, bringing a vernacular touch to more desolate locales, are *hai-makura*. Across the planet, in nearly every culture, folklore details how poetry resides in distinct places—particularly the remote, isolated, dangerous, inaccessible. The headwaters of a creek, the high grassy meadow flattened by wind. One goes for adventure, danger, solitude; to practice a strict discipline or to seek advice from the torrents of nature.

It is precious to have a lover go with you. It is ecological to give something in return. A song, a poem, a prayer, a joke.

Oh yes, a joke.

5 November

Incense has dispersed from the hall,
the blue-winged birds have departed.
Autumn comes to the Hou precipices & the jade
pipe grows faint.

Jingwei wrote these lines in 17th century China. Late autumn is for melancholy. A fragrance of wet leaf mould stirred with fermenting apples. I have a body that evolved in the Pleistocene & want to burrow under the covers. This is the season for love. Distressing article on coal-bed methane drilling: the implications for ground water toxicity along the Rocky Mountains. Her poem finishes—

Now the human realm, alone
in the robes of a nun.

6 November

The plot of land under the oak is honeycombed with tight
passways & treeroots. Are they connected to some initiatory process? I'm scared
to descend through the convoluted, the branching
chambers of limestone.

Guilt hangs over the dream. In Japan a female fox winds through the grass. The withered grass, the chill & lonely wind. Wild onions. The men lose their spirits and disappear. Jonathan Cohen is staring into the entrance. He prepares to go down, heavily, without enthusiasm, simply to show it can be done. I'm reminded of spirals on the passage graves of the Boyne Valley. Jon is clearly an animal guide in my psyche—in waking life a psychoanalyst who works at the "thinking cure." But the guilt is what—?

Dawn: tins of paint
& a slightly burnt candle
—the autumn fox fades

Wabi-cha is to be outwardly poor, folksy, off-kilter. To go in worn clothes into Indian Peaks. No hi-tech gear. To be chipped. A bit cracked.

41

7 November

Awakening to the high, returning to the low. All I ever wanted for poetry.

Or: "…if what you feel in your heart is ten,
what appears should be seven."
—Zeami

8 November

Looking through files I found this five year old letter
run in The Daily Camera—

OPEN FORUM   /   10 November 1998

Editors,

    Not just the news media, but mainstream environmental groups have branded the ELFs who burnt two ski lifts and a restaurant at Vail "terrorists." Isn't it industrial recreation that constitutes the terrorist force though? Corporate interests despoil wilderness that is owned by the public, and at Vail is destroying the final habitat of the Rocky Mountain lynx. Commercial skiing, snowmobiles, dirt bikes, high-tech climbing, and other activities involving elaborate and costly equipment have replaced timber and mining as the forces most destructive of wild lands and threatened species in our state. It seems that as long as ecology activists do not disrupt the basic workings of international Capital their views are tolerated. When activists refuse to permit public lands to be despoiled by industry, even those who should be their allies betray them.

    Right now in Colorado the White River National Forest Service is looking at management plans for its holdings. The Service's preferred Alternative D would restrict ski resorts and real estate development to current boundaries, including throughout the Vail basin and along the I-70 corridor. It would remove illegal roads, declare tens of thousands of acres unsuited for mechanized travel, and manage the forest for biodiversity and ecosystem health. For maybe the first time, a division of the Forest Service is showing a resolve more far-reaching than you find in the Sierra Club. Martha Kettele, the new White River chief, needs support as she tries to limit industrial recreation.

    Her opponents? The usual cast: Senators with campaign coffers filled by developers, off-road equipment manufacturers, and irresponsible folk with too much cash who imagine our planet their playground.

Andrew Schelling
Jack Kerouac School of Disembodied Poetics
The Naropa Institute

11 November

An entry, 3 January, *Pine Linen Notebook*
> *nirukti-pratisamvid*
> "knower of languages"
>> one attribute of the bodhisattva

And in southern Africa about thirty "click languages" survive. Thought to be "very old" they belong to an ancient genetic line, the *Ju | 'hoansi* (upright bar indicates a click). Outside Africa the only language known to use clicks was Damin, an extinct aboriginal tongue of Australia taught to men for initiatory rites.

> "The divergence of these genetic lineages is among the oldest on earth, so one would certainly make the inference that clicks were present in the Mother tongue."

The call, the cry, the whimper, the growl, the moan, the click, the bay—
we sighed & cooed softly
> migrating alongside other mammals

My sister-in-law hurries across the deck & discharges her pistol towards the pack. The sky is feathered with sunset. Up the hillside the wolves scatter—lean, gray & black. They have torn a small dog but did not violate our compound. The fear is that as languages go extinct, precise possibilities & lore, even intricate sciences, vanish with them. A sound like the cracking of branches.

> "Clicks are acoustically high-impact sounds for mammalian ears, probably the worst sounds if you are trying to conceal your presence."

13 November

Winds of late autumn took much of the shed's roofing. Scraps of tarpaper, newspaper, leaf mulch, & squirrel-gnawed apples. 8:00 a.m. sun in cold, lowlying clouds. On the table I've arranged *Diamond Sutra* papers for 12:30 class. In melancholy temper the mind reflects on half a lifetime put into Sanskrit—lamplit nights, Santa Cruz Mountains—incessant rain in the redwoods—leaning over Monier-Williams' massive blue dictionary.

The first translations. First thoughts of goddess language, *Giram Devi*. I pictured

her by the riverbank & wrote my first published poem. It closed with a prayer to her.
Solitary discoveries, esoteric nightbound joys. Cold mist in the gorge. In a wooden
shack the archaic craft in large part learnt from this dear volume's 1332 pages—

Kosha

a cask, a vessel for liquids
(metaphorically, clouds)
a drinking vessel, a cup
box, cupboard, drawer, trunk
sheath,
a scabbard
a case, cover, a covering
store-room, store, or provisions
a treasury;
treasure, accumulated wealth
apartment where money or plate is kept
gold or silver wrought or unwrought
a dictionary, lexicon or vocabulary
a poetic collection
collection of sentences
bud, flower-cup, seed vessel
the sheath or integument of a plant, pod, or nut-shell
the inner part of a fruit
silk worm cocoon
the membrane covering an egg in the womb
the vulva
testicle or scrotum
the penis
a term for the three sheathes or succession of cases which make
up the various frames of the body enveloping the soul:
"sheath of pleasure"
"sheath of intellect"
"sheath of nourishment"
the second astrological mansion
an oath; nutmeg;
an iron plough share;
the beard of corn

This *kosha*, dictionary, traded twenty-five years ago from a friend I've lost track of. Now it too is longtime companion. It has outlasted: nine households, two journeys through Asia, six trips in Mexico; two marriages, three sets of hiking boots, five automobiles, four jobs, three Sierra cups, six tea pots. Guide through 400 poems, comrade to two Buddhist sutras & nine Upanishads. Epics magic & war-driven; Jayadeva & Kalidasa's cycles of love; one frightful Tantra; King Hala's 700 *gathas* of peasant & tribal lore. Tangled muscle serpent syntax, dark speculative wings, predator tooth; eye glint & glands of musk; seeds of hair-raising insight—

> January 27th, 1988   12:53 a.m.
> Althea
> unsheathed herself from the womb.
> The book gave us an image—
> *shasha-lakshana*
>
> "the hare-marked moon"

15 November

The most prosaic dream, nearly indistinguishable from waking perception, proves on closer study to contain some incongruous element: something mad, ill-fitting, magical, distressingly out of place. It may occur in the image or just out of sight. When the gods took human form they kept some trace or whiff of the animal—a tiny beast face peers under the headdress from the pile of hair.

Now I discover the eye of an insect's always compound. The dragonfly's has 30,000 facets. A fly processes images into "readable movies" five times quicker than human sight. It moves at crazy speeds & doesn't collide.

> Night of horned acorn moon—
> wind torrents took the shed's
> roofing off.

16 November

Snow banners trail from North Arapaho today. "The dead end of remaking the gods in human form." And at Kinko's, copying *Claw Moraine* for Christine Holland, a handwritten scrap of paper was lying on the worktable—

> "So it's a tragic ending
> to our "tail" of hope.
>
> Ursula Snowcone was
> captured, Kaka &
> Jennitalia sabotaged our
> message, but Debbie-does-
> the-best-She-can will
> continue her mission.
> Unfortunately for her we
> know there is no end."

> *(here the paper was carefully torn)*

Now nearly weeping need a drink—the wild, wreck'd loves of our past— & into the night.

*   *

Took the new axe, split & stacked a few weeks supply of wood. Ten years or twenty since I got my heat from a woodstove? The sharp burnt smell when the axe-head falls cleanly through. In California I'd haul anything out of the hills—"wood stew." Madrone, bay laurel, oak, pine, old two-by-fours, logs with moss hanging off, even redwood. Cottonwood's the redwood of the high plains: tough, fibrous, hard to split, lousy to burn. Lucky to have elm, juniper, ponderosa, maple, & some much-coveted fruit wood— compact, bitter smoke; & good hard coals.

> "L'Art est long et le Temp est court," says Baudelaire.
> The perfection of wood-splitting a life-long study—?

Know your gear, know your tools. Part of the fun of going into the mountains is the strict material discipline. The limited elements, their potential fury. Turtle fur catastrophe hat in case of snow, my knife handle's unbreakable rabbit horn.

Given a choice, most humans would select a dwelling site on a bit of a rise. Give me a view above the trees, across the savanna; & access to water. Inclinations formed in the Pleistocene, along with powerful eyesight & a mind that looks into other worlds. I want plenty of firewood. At night, staring into the embers, your whole life seems to go past, clinking across the coals. Jorna Bose phoned from Paris to talk about Deben's anthology of 20th century Bengali poems. He'd sent me a copy three weeks before dying—no note attached.

"Deben lived like a Baul—" Jorna says; the wild-haired Bengal street singers he translated, "—with no attachments. The one thing he loved though was his collection of tapes." Songs recorded in the field & along the rivers of India since 1954.

gadget: a small specialized mechanical or electronic device, a contrivance.

*   *

From Deben's *Chandidas*—

"I throw dust on all laws made by men or gods"

18 November

In a former lifetime the Buddha was born a hare. He happened on a group of luckless starving hunters who were trying to make stew out of dry grass. *What else would I do with this useless body?* ...and threw himself into the pot.

> "For that merciful deed I'll make you visible
> to all on earth"
> scoring his image on the autumn moon's disk—

"The hare marked moon."

21 November

Althea arrived this evening. Tall and willowy, at the airport she grabbed me from behind. And the dream of the night she was born swept back.

> A deserted track through crackling chaparral, me traveling alone.
> Some animal cry lifts from a near clump of bushes, *ceanothus*—
> those tight, blue-budded wild lilacs of California. My impulse is
> to run—hair bristling—but something restrains me. I turn in time
> to glimpse in the dusk some flitting shape under the thicket. A
> whimper—and lift my face from the pillow to find her, helpless-
> looking, a tiny bundle wrapped in a receiving blanket, utterly
> alone in the expansive center of bed. She's giving off the dream's
> animal whimpers. I fold her in my arms & sleep until daybreak—

Repeated dreams of my daughter. I need to provide safety, shelter, nourishment. How guide her through a world of bewildering forces? Keep her from the mistakes I made? Another dream with her my companion—threats of guitars & weapons in a dark unfamiliar neighborhood overgrown with leafy bushes—we possess a car, mattresses, and deerskin gloves, all necessary to drop into a dirt-floor provision cellar, stacked with firewood and winter fruit. We are safe in the storage cellar, thanks to the tawny deerskin gloves, their palms grimy—

A notebook to put ghosts to rest.
A notebook for withered late autumn grass.
Snow banner notebook. High country notebook of glacier cut pages.
Notebook subduing the cold,
   shelter the couch of love notebook—
Can a notebook rectify
long-standing wrongs? Teach the children
our goodness, their animal bodies, graces & ecstasies—
but warn them from our own mistakes?
Has anyone the courage, the deftness, to correct
   such things in a notebook?

22 November

A light, dancing snow, driven by wind.

Visited the bookstore with Althea and she came away with a stack of titles. One function of poetry, to amuse the living. Another, to gratify the dead. How dark, how inconsiderate, that until last week I had not written even a line of verse for Deben. Might I have lost his manuscript? I will provide another, across the thin membrane that separates worlds. This time of year it's particularly thin. There is praise for one's host; then there is praise for the land. Finally one makes an offering to the dead. It is not scary—

Haii: the spirit of haikai

First it meant comic: distinct from the narrow seriousness of classical verse. In Basho's practice it broadened. It came to mean innovative, anti-traditional, opposed to convention. It introduced vernacular words, colloquial phrases, & Chinese compounds. Buddhist terminology & popular sayings came in. To find unvisited language zones, new emotions, a new vegetation—

  "defamiliarizing and refamiliarizing the cultural landscape"

Snow along the rough angled limb of the Russian olive.

24 November

I am the notorious ghost. A rust-orange robe covers me. But someone determines I need a padded white under-gown. When I get fitted there are two striking women, one with burnished skin, pale nipples, and blond fur on her belly. I lie my face against her stomach but the other girl humiliates me with debasing gestures—

       … & I've entered the provision room for the monastery with Robert: shelves of candles, incense, ceremonial cloth, & waxy vegetables or fruit strung along dry corded vines. Hard to tell the gnarled, misshapen candles from the dark green skin of the fruit or long peppers. One monk taking inventory says what appear to be candles are fruit.

       Is this the *alaya-vijnana*? the "storehouse consciousness" of the Yogacara philosophers? The roof is draped with maroon & saffron, and prayer flags line the walls. Have I come to the vast empty hall from which all seeds emerge—?

25 November

Harvest days. The gathering of the year. The stacking of fruit & firewood. This year I will take heat only from wood, coal-bed methane extraction being such a disaster. The buried seams crack under pressure, the retort like an earthquake, and noxious gas enters the water table. From the *Diamond Sutra,* in class we arrived at this for *sattva-samgraha*: assembly of beings. *Whoever can be collected in the assembly of beings.*

       I roast a chicken for Althea and Marlow. This book is for them. The old terms of kinship no longer fit our complicated loves. Maple & apple branches I take from the woodpile once grew on long-vanished trees up the alley. We light the stove—

     *   *

Dear Mary,

      Winds are battering the stove pipe. September was snow-less, no snow came in October. Finally last week a windy & very decisive blizzard. Night winds took most of the snow from the yard, but the roads remain icy, the mercury low.

      And yesterday I was musing with Althea over the books of her childhood. How free they were! I suppose what makes a children's book glow is simplicity. It does no good the writer be smart, only wily. Does this mean authentic? Good night moon may be the best line ever written. Then came the Oz books, which I grew up on—as Robert Duncan did—a tradition I passed to Althea. Funny, in my dreams he & Althea can still appear as the same figure after a gap of fifteen years—him dead the week she was born, her a willful teenager now.

      We may have read only six or seven Oz books, but ten years back started collecting them. We'd been visiting Bob and Susan Arnold in Vermont & saw their son Carson's collection. It was a book-case of mystery-relics. After that Althea wanted one Oz for Christmas, one for her birthday, year after year.

      The first mature book in her life was Jaime's *Indian Tales* though. She quickly got that Coyote Old Man was her grandfather. "He's everybody's grandfather!" the ant people cry in derision. But Althea had the birth-mark, right on the wrist where her grandfather had it. Coyote slunk vividly near, his tail flat out behind. We would go to a mountain roadhouse in Nederland for lunch; her grandfather had done the wood work & the little stained glass window I told her. We knew he'd fled into the spruce hills when finished, yelping at his own mischief. "Ululating."

      Now winter comes on, & it is more than delightful to lie in bed listening to the wind, or rise in the dark and peer at the stars. Orion at 3:00 a.m. stands right overhead, sword tilted a bit towards Green Mountain. Behind, silently, the grave summits of the Indian Peaks. They give the tooth fairy her bearings. At least in Althea's childhood they did. From down here, after replacing the tooth under the pillow with silver, she would fly towards their sawtooth ridges, facing the evening star, then with a leftward turn direct herself for Tibet.

      After that it was "straight on till morning."

                    With all love,
                        Andrew

Fox lurking in the night
I see your eyes.
Go tell the waxing moon
That my mind is dark.

—Jaime de Angulo
"Shaman Songs"

Andrew Schelling, born 14 January, 1953. Thirteen books of poetry, essays, and translation. Mountain excursions, natural history, bioregion; poetry of classical India; on-the-hoof prowling. Recent titles include *Tea Shack Interior: New & Selected Poetry*, and a collection of essays, *Wild Form, Savage Grammar*. Editor of *The Wisdom Anthology of North American Buddhist Poetry*. Currently researching Jaime de Angulo for a book on wilderness and West Coast Literature. Lives with his daughter Althea in the Southern Rocky Mountain ecosystem and teaches poetry and Sanskrit at Naropa University in Boulder, Colorado.

BOOTSTRAP IS . . .

Bootstrap Productions is a 501 (c) 3 non-profit publishing company that promotes the integration of multi-dimensional art forms and experiments into fine press publishing.

The organization seeks to introduce the general public to experimental and contemporary art and writing; to stimulate public interest in the work of new, struggling and relatively unknown artists; and to benefit the community generally by promoting the appreciation of contemporary art and writing.

The organization's goal is to provide a venue that affords the benefits and aesthetics of a quality small press to committed and brilliant writers, visual artists, and musicians who may not otherwise have the opportunity and freedom to display their work as they envision it.

The organization creates the opportunity for the public to experience and learn about such art and writing that might otherwise never have a public forum.

Two Elk: A High Country Notebook was printed Summer 2005 in an edition of 1000 copies by McNaughton & Gunn of Saline, Michigan, of which 26 are signed and lettered A-Z by the poet.

As a commitment to the author's eco-conscious work, this book was printed on recycled paper with soy-based inks.